I Ha

I Hate Potatoes

They Make Me Cry

Boonmee Pakviset McElroy, MSW, LICSW, CLC

ISBN: 978-1-945446-93-1

I dedicate this book to my late parents: Mr. Charee Pakviset, my father, who is passionate about Thai Boxing. He is a man with charm, charisma, and character. My mother, Mrs. Soon Pakviset, without whom I would not have had the opportunity to live this fabulous life. I love you, Mom, and I love you, Dad. I wish that you are watching and celebrating my wonderful life with me. I hope and pray that you are both watching over me, my husband, and my beautiful sons, Micah Charee McElroy and Marcus Kenneth McElroy.

I also dedicate this book to my brother, Nopthunsak Pakviset (Mhee), who saw my true potential, loved me unconditionally, and protected me from all the bullies. My brother is a man with charm, charisma, courage, and a kind heart.

I love you and I am always grateful for your support.

Praise for
I Hate Potatoes

"This book sheds light on the issues of abuse, poverty, and trauma while showing how anyone can overcome them when they find their true purpose through hope and faith."

—Bob Proctor, Transformational Speaker,
NY Times Bestselling Author, and
Featured Teacher from the Hit Movie, *The Secret*

"Our own happiness has been clouded by the concept of *more*... more material goods, more money, more notoriety... so much so that we have lost track of our purpose. *I Hate Potatoes* reminds us of what is most important: to find our purpose and remain hopeful in the pursuit of it."

— Jessica Sander, Art Director, T Brand,
The New York Times

"This inspiring book makes a unique connection between poverty and trauma while demonstrating the ultimate triumph of overcoming both."

—Keith Leon S., 5 x Award Winning,
8 x International Bestselling Author,
Publisher, and Motivational Speaker

"In *I Hate Potatoes,* Boonmee's lived experiences and life lessons, which she shares powerfully by being vulnerable, will carry on with you forever."

—Nelsie Yang, City Council Member
of Ward 6 in St. Paul, Minnesota

"Boonmee's powerful story of her traumatic journey from Thailand is moving and inspiring. She shares difficulties she endured and illuminates a path to a hopeful future by calling for kindness and commitment to purpose."

—Virginia M. Wright-Peterson, Author of
Women of Mayo Clinic: The Founding Generation
and *A Woman's War, Too:*
Women at Work During WWII

"Boonmee's journey in *I Hate Potatoes* shows you that there is light at the end of the tunnel, and provides a road map to finding your own inner source of power and purpose."

—Rachel Davis, PhD,
International Leadership Coach and Author

"We have lost track of our own happiness by being so obsessed with material goods, more money, and more fame... so much so that purpose goes out the window. Once in a while, a gift is presented to us that brings us back to what's most important. *I Hate Potatoes* is that gift."

—Julie Senska, Licensed Counselor at Byron High School in Byron, Minnesota

"Through the vivid description of steamed wild potatoes, I, too, taste the pain of poverty and childhood adversities, yet *I Hate Potatoes* also shares incredible insights filled with love and hope that were born out of overcoming hardships."

—Yuko Taniguchi, Author of *Foreign Wife Elegy,* and *The Ocean in the Closet*

"By bravely and candidly sharing her life's journey from loss, hurt, and hardship to hope, healing and inner peace, Boonmee will inspire and help others discover their inner beauty, wisdom, and life's purpose."

— Nancy Fitzsimons, PhD, MSW, LISW, Professor at Minnesota State University Mankato, Department of Social Work, and Author

"In *I Hate Potatoes,* Boonmee offers us a beautiful window into the diverse lived experiences of South Asian immigrants in the U.S. Her inspiring story of strength and resilience reminds us that hope, healing, and wellbeing are always within reach."

—Andrew Williams, MA, Director of Diversity, Equity, and Inclusion at the Betty Ford Hazelden Foundation

"This book draws a road map for finding life purpose through perseverance and faith. In this book, Boonmee's deepest desire is to share how a shift of focus from the distractions of the outside world, to instead, your inner world, will lead you to your purpose, which is your true source of wisdom, joy and peace. This book is truly magical. The real-life stories that help Boonmee discover her path and purpose are rich, authentic and heartfelt. You will find inspiration on every page. It's a must-read!"

—Lisa Winston, #1 International Bestselling Author, TV Host, Inspirational Speaker, and Artist

Contents

Foreword

"The author offers an interesting exploration of the development of cognitive distortions and limiting beliefs about the self, as she tells the story of her life experiences.

Knowing the author personally, her naturally sweet spirit and hard-won wisdom are evident as she writes about the challenges and traumas of her life in a way that encourages the reader to understand the shared humanity of such lived experience.

Using her training as a cognitive-behavioral therapist, she is able to show how life can both teach us to believe we are 'less than' we really are, as well as how those thoughts and beliefs can be challenged and overcome."

— Betsy Bateman, Licensed Psychologist
in St. Paul, Minnesota

Acknowledgments

I thank my husband, Mike McElroy, for his love and support with this project and throughout our relationship. Thank you for being a wonderful husband to me and an awesome father to our children. I also acknowledge my two beautiful boys, Micah and Marcus McElroy, who have encouraged me and inspired me to be my best self. I extend my gratitude to my in-laws, Mike and Kathy McElroy, for being such loving and caring grandparents to my sons.

I especially acknowledge my brother for being by my side through thick and thin, for being my real-life hero who saw my true potential. Thank you for always protecting me and looking after me with such admiration and caring. I thank you for always supporting me, protecting me, encouraging me, and sharing my journey with me. I love you, Mhee (Nopthunsak Pakviset).

I would like to thank my Empath and Forever Friend Martha Daniels for her support and validation of my work.

I would like to express my gratitude to the YouSpeakIt Book program for easing my anxiety of writing my first book and making it as painless as possible.

Special thank-you especially to Maura and Keith Leon for believing in me and my story.

Special thanks to the team of writers and editors at the YouSpeakItBook program, especially Rona and Nida. Rona provided me a sense of ease and calm when sharing my story. Her listening skills and her validation of my story made a difference. I would like to thank Nida for always facilitating timely communication to keep me on schedule.

Introduction

I wrote this book with the intention to instill hope and kindness in humankind. I feel that in the past decade, our society has become consumed by negatives. We have also become superficial with one another. We have lived in a world full of distractions, somehow conditioned to look for more material goods, more money, and more fame. We have more of everything under the sun but happiness and purpose.

At some point, I heard on a radio show that 85 percent of the American people are not happy at their job. Imagine this—we spend more than 80 percent of our waking hours at the workplace, and we are not happy with our jobs.

Does this mean we are also not happy in our personal lives?

It is sad we have somehow lost track of our own happiness, hope, and faith. I want this book to be a reminder that happiness, hope, and faith are still around you and within you. My aim is to help you focus less on the distractions of the material world and go inward to get in touch with your own wisdom and purpose. This book assists you as you focus again on happiness, hope, and faith—and perhaps slow down and pay attention to all the blessings given to us: food, shelter, clean water, medicines, advanced technology, and access to education. We have everything and every reason to be happy and joyful. Let us start enjoying ourselves and be kind toward one another and start living life with purpose.

I am a woman, a mother of two beautiful boys, Micah, three years old, and Marcus, two years old. I am a wife. I am a mental health counselor. I am a sister, an auntie, a healer, a life coach, and an inspirational speaker. I am here to spread love, kindness, hope, and happiness and to inspire people to live life with purpose.

I am here to remind you about the gift of life, the gift of faith. So, that is the reason I want to share my life story. I will consider my book successful if I make a difference in at least one person's life. I also hope that one day, when my sons become adults, they will know their mom's life journey and, informed by it, live their life with purpose and joy. I wish for my boys to feel inspired by the message in this book and hope that they, too, will find their own true purpose and true happiness in life. I am excited to witness them growing up, becoming good citizens, and making a difference in the world.

The best way to read this book is to read it with curiosity and compassion. Read it as though you are about to be invited into somebody's life—especially the most vulnerable moments of a person's life. I want you to embrace this opportunity and feel the impact of my story. While you read this book, I ask you to hold that curiosity, compassion, and open-mindedness.

I hope that, in some way, this book will serve as reminder for you to start enjoying and celebrating your life. If you want to, of course, read with a notebook and pen at hand to note what inspires you, what sticks with you, what resonates with you, or what you can relate to in some way. Write it down. It might mean something later. You could create a book club and connect with other readers.

Allow yourself to be vulnerable; allow yourself to explore your own journey with this book. It could shed some light on your true purpose, on your life path. Perhaps this book could evoke some passion, inspiration, encouragement, motivation, hope, forgiveness, and kindness. My wish for you is to start living your life to the fullest, to celebrate your blessings, and to pursue your dreams!

CHAPTER ONE

Welcome to the Family

WHO AM I?

At a young age, I had a sense of feeling as though I was *not enough* in some ways. I felt not enough as a woman and not enough as a person. I believe this sense stemmed from the lack of a relationship with my mom, since she passed away when I was five years old. I did not have a sense of belonging. I did not know who I was as a child, or what I was like.

The first memory I have of my mother is of the day she passed. I remember watching villagers come to my house. There was a ritual in which people were bathing my mom's body. At the time, I did not understand the meaning of death or dying. It was an odd experience. I watched them cleaning my mom's body, and that was it. That is all I remember of my mother.

I regret I did not have the mother-and-daughter kind of experience. At that time, I formed a belief that perhaps I was sinful and that was why I had a sense of not belonging—because I lost my mom so soon, so early in my life. I do not have any memory of her at all, other than that picture in my memory. So that is where my sense of not belonging comes from.

Of course, as an older person looking back, I know it is not my fault, and it was not her fault that she passed away so young. Still, I cannot help but feel bad and guilty for not having any memory of her. Every time people asked me: What does your mom look like? What is she like? I could not answer, but there was one thing my siblings would tell me every time I asked about my mom.

They would say: *If you want to know what your mother looks like, go stand in front of a mirror.*

I didn't understand what that meant until later in life. She must have looked just like me. So I must look just like her. And that is the only thing I have of my mom—knowing that I look like her. But somehow, I still do not feel *I am enough.*

Fundamentally, I have always felt alone. Because I did not know who I came from, I did not know who I was; therefore, I did not know what to fall back on when things went wrong. I knew her name, but I did not have any memory or experience of being with my mother. I am so sad when I think about it. It is so cold when I think about relationships, when I think about how I do not have that connection with my mom.

When people say: *Tell me about your parents,* or when people have lost their loved ones or their mom, especially, I feel so guilty because I do not know how to relate; I do not know how to empathize with people who have lost their mom. For the longest time, it has not fit right with me because I do not feel authentic. I do not feel real when I say: *I am so sorry for your loss.* It sounds good; it sounds like the polite thing to say, but deep down in my heart, I do not know what that feels like.

I felt like a liar saying those things to people who had lost their mom—remarks like: *I am sorry for your loss.* I knew I was saying the right thing, but I struggled to relate to that pain. It seems ironic because I lost my mom, too, but I never had her in my life. I have a hard time still.

Sometimes I ask myself: *If I had a chance to go back in time to connect to my mom, what would I say to her?*

I do not know what I would ask her first, second, or third. There are no questions that come to mind. I feel such a sense of . . . nothingness. I do not even know if I should feel angry about that or sad about that. This issue has continued. I tell myself perhaps I am not a good person, perhaps I am not a good woman, perhaps I will not be able to be a good mom because I do not have that experience or a role model to look up to.

So that is my struggle with connecting to my own mother or a mother figure in my life. I feel there is something more about this, but I do not know what it is yet. I am now a mom myself, so I think this experience has slowly healed me, has healed that area of my life.

False Self-Beliefs

Looking back to the moment I witnessed on the day my mom passed, I reflect upon my thought process as a five-year-old girl. I did not know what I was observing. I did not know what death meant nor did I know about the funeral ritual I was witnessing, and there was a sense of: *Something is very wrong here!* Of course, as a five-year-old, with a five-year old's brain, I thought: *I am the center of the universe; therefore, I must fix the feeling that something is wrong here.* I figured I had to make everything better, so I somehow decided to entertain people and acted bubbly and cheerful while the villagers cleaned my mom's body.

I think that was the moment I developed my first identity, which later turned into my personality.

Guess who I have become later in life?

A bubbly, cheerful, life of the party. That identity was developed out of the failure to be *enough* to compensate for what was happening in front of me. Somehow that experience has continued to show up in my life throughout my adulthood. Whenever things do not go well, or when bad things happen to me, I fall back into the belief that because *I am not enough,* bad things happened to me. *I am not enough to make my own mother stay, so I must be a sinful person.*

So that belief has been the punching bag for me, if you will. I tend to lean in to that story to make things okay and make sense out of things. Subconsciously, I kept telling myself this story over and over. It is funny how the mind works. I guess it was easier for me to tell myself the story that I am a sinful person and do not deserve good things, do not deserve to be loved. I assumed this mindset wouldn't affect me as an adult because I would become wiser and know fact versus fiction, but I was wrong.

This false belief continued to dictate my behaviors and my actions. For instance, I tend to doubt when good things happen to me. I tend to question people's intentions and motives, and I do not trust anyone easily. This subconscious belief has sabotaged many relationships and caused emotional turmoil. It has caused me to feel lonely and alone for a very long time.

HUNGER IS PAIN

Another dominant memory associated with my childhood was hunger. My experience of being hungry has shaped the way I think about food, and it has shaped the way I look at life in a variety of ways.

Growing up, after my mom's death, there was my brother and me. My memory of that time is that I was hungry because we never had enough food. We never knew when we would get the next meal or if we would eat again. It was a constant worry about food, about eating. Would our dad come home with food? Just the experience of uncertainty, the experience of not knowing whether we would have another meal, was hard to understand at a young age.

At the same time, I didn't know any other way of life to compare my experience to. We grew up in a small village with no electricity, no nothing. You did not witness anybody else's life, so all we knew was our own experience and our own world. With that, I do not know if it was a good thing or bad thing to not realize how poor we were compared to others. All I remember was that I felt hungry all the time.

All day long, my mind was consumed by thoughts surrounding food: *I need to eat food. I do not know if I am going to have food today or tomorrow.* I would imagine eating food.

Hunger was painful.

I remember going to school. It was a small school with fewer than four hundred students. At lunch time, Teacher would ring the big old bell. All the kids would run out of the classroom and go into the lunch area, in a separate building.

I never had any lunch with me, so I formed an odd behavior, which was to make myself sleep during lunchtime. The ringing of the bell was a signal for me to fall asleep because I could not bear the thought of sitting next to other kids eating their lunch. The hunger would be too unbearable. So I conditioned my brain to instantly fall asleep. I would just curl up like a ball under my desk and pretend nobody could see me.

I do not know how long I had been running that racket to avoid embarrassment. I do not know which fear was worse: the fear of feeling the pain of hunger or the fear of feeling embarrassed by someone seeing me with no food. It was the only solution that a five-year-old could come up with. I would sleep and hide in my classroom until everyone came back to class, and I would pretend I had been in the lunchroom earlier. I think my teacher caught up to my scam, so she shared her lunch with me occasionally. But the experience of hunger has remained prominent in my life.

I Hate Potatoes

I wanted to share this funny story, though it was not funny at that time.

Growing up in Thailand, our main food or staple was rice. Rice is a symbol of prosperity and abundance. My father supposedly had a lot of land, but he was not the kind of person who enjoyed doing hard labor. So we never had enough rice in our house—at least, if we did, it never lasted long.

So my dad would find wild potatoes. They are not like the regular potatoes we eat in the United States. They are taro potatoes, wild potatoes, that we'd dig up in the woods somewhere. My father would chop them into small pieces and steam them, and that was it. That was our meal.

It became a common meal for us because Dad did not want to do the hard, physical labor of growing rice or farming. He had his own passion, which was Muay Thai (Thai boxing). He would travel on foot from city to city and province to province. At times, he would come home with a bag of rice, which meant that he won a match. Sometimes, all he came home with was a lot of bruises. Anyway, our main food was wild potatoes. Sometimes we would eat steamed potatoes for days in a row, and that's why *I hate potatoes!*

Fast-forward to my teenage years. I was living in Bangkok city at that time, and I was able to make my own money. I went to the farmers' market, and I was stunned to find *goddamned steamed wild potatoes!* for sale. I started crying at the sight of them, but I could not articulate the reason.

The feeling of disgust was so strong that I did not want to have even one bite of a steamed potato for the rest of my life. In fact, potatoes reminded me of how hungry I was and how poor I was. That was the reason I did not eat potatoes.

The memory of hunger remains at the back of my mind whenever I see people waste food, when I see children have a whole plate of food in front of them that they do not want to eat, so they toss it. It is an ongoing battle, an internal conflict, for me to see our lives become so wasteful in this culture. We do not respect food the way I grew up respecting it.

It continues to play a big role in my life, even today. I remember the first Thanksgiving meal with my spouse's family. They only enjoyed the white meat of a turkey. They were about to toss the rest of the bird, full of dark meat, in the trash.

I said, "Oh please, do not do that. I would save that."

In my mind, I could see that I could turn the dark meat into another dish or give it to homeless people.

But the response I heard from my father-in-law was, "Oh, you want to eat *the scraps?*"

For some reason, that hurt me deeply. I felt so disrespected; I felt so insulted by that comment. I felt again that I was not good enough because scraps are trash, and I had suggested eating something that most people look down upon. I felt offended by that comment for a long time.

On a side note, I feel that we in the United States are wasteful. We have no clue of how privileged our lives are. It makes me angry when I see people be so dismissive, when they overlook how readily available food is and take life for granted. It continues to be an issue of mine when it comes to food and food waste.

This culture seems to take for granted access to food, water, shelter, and clothes. People do not seem to realize how important this easy access is. It reminds me of my first culture shock regarding food when I came to the United States. I saw kids have an entire meal (half a chicken, which could feed the entire family in my hometown) all to themselves. It still surprises me because it took me years before I could afford to have an entire drumstick all to myself.

Where I grew up, one chicken leg or a chicken thigh could feed a family of five. We would chop the meat—any kind of meat that we gathered—finely and put it into a big pot of soup with a lot of vegetables. Soup is the only way you can feed a big family with minimal resources. So now, when I see kids have an entire bird to themselves, or a whole a chicken breast, or a chicken thigh, I think: How is that possible? How can this small person have an entire piece of chicken to themselves, when we fed the whole family with the same amount? Children here can pick and choose what part of the bird they want to eat, what part they enjoy, and what part they do not. It still blows my mind.

Do we realize what a luxury it is to pick and choose what we are going to eat?

That experience was not laughable back then. I slowly have come to learn and adapt to a new lifestyle. I guess life does hold a lot of inequality. When you come from the side of the world I came from, it is hard to witness people throwing away food and not appreciating what they have.

One of my life aspirations is to cease hunger. I want to find a way to end wasting food and produce. Grocery stores from everywhere dispose of billions of pounds of edible food a year. Much of that waste is actually usable. We could feed the entire planet from that. Yet somehow, we haven't figured this out. And we live in the greatest country. I still cannot wrap my head around this.

Why have we not done this?

If I become rich, that will be my first project: end hunger for all.

WELCOME TO THE FAMILY

I lived two different childhoods, two different beginnings, to my life. When I was seven years old, my dad decided to move us to a different city, called Kalasin, which I had never heard of. He introduced me and my brother to whole bunch of people. Some of those people were in their forties, some in their thirties, some in their twenties. We met a bunch of people, and I had no clue who they were.

Our dad said, "These are your siblings."

My reality, the world I was born into, changed. I did not realize that my father had so many children before us. *How can I not know any of this?* I wondered. Although my other siblings claimed they knew about my brother and me, in my own memory, I never met them before. That was the first time I met my half-siblings.

Some were welcoming; some were not welcoming. But I did not understand any of that. Everything was so confusing. Our dad didn't say much. He just told us these were our siblings, and we were going to be with them now. I felt so small, I guess. I felt smaller than a person. There were a bunch of other people before me.

I had thought it was just me and my brother, and that I was the center of the world. But when my dad introduced me to the rest of his children, *my siblings,* I felt so small. I thought: *I am not the center of his life anymore.*

An Unwanted Burden

The first year we were introduced to my half-siblings, things were fine and everything seemed normal. One sibling, my new sister, Sopha, was the middle child of ten children from my father's first marriage. She would sometimes act like a loving and caring sister. But she soon showed that she did not want us to be a part of their lives.

I had never had that experience before—perhaps because I was so young. I felt like I was a burden. She never had good things to say about us, and she tried not to have much interaction when our dad was around. But when my father was not around, or when he turned his back, she would pull my hair, hit me on the head, or say demeaning things.

At my young age, I did not understand what some of her words meant, but I knew she did not like me. She would tell me I was the reason why her father, who was also our father, was absent in her life. All sorts of things like this happened, and I was confused. I felt as if Sopha did not want me there. So, moving there caused me to feel like a burden.

I believe this is the moment when I formed the belief: *I am a burden to people.*

Photo credit: Ryan Balow

CHAPTER TWO

Does Anyone See or Hear Me?

THE ABANDONMENT

A couple years after we moved in with our half-siblings, we learned that Dad was sick, but nobody knew about until it was too late. He was on bed rest for a couple months it seemed. I was about to turn ten years old.

I came home from school one day and noticed a lot of villagers were gathered at my house to visit my dad, I guess. I approached and saw my father lying in bed. At the time, I did not know what illness my father had. Where we lived in Thailand, at that time, people lived their lives in their own little world. We did not have access to medical care. We did not have access to medication. We'd just get sick and eventually die.

In my memory, my father was sick, and then he simply died. I remember crying, but I also remember feeling numb and confused. I did not know what to think; I did not know what to say. I had this feeling of emptiness. I remember the world was so quiet and seemed to stand still. I had never experienced anything like that before.

Within a few days after Dad died, my abusive sister started to control my life. I felt angry, and at the time, with a ten-year-old's brain, I had no idea how to comprehend what had happened to me. Somehow I made the connection that, as soon as my father died, bad things started to happen to me. At that young age, the only way I could make sense of what was happening and survive that painful time was to blame something or someone.

I now know my dad probably did not want to die, but at that young age, all I could make of it was that he left me to suffer. I did not fully recognize until later that, deep down, I blamed my father for leaving me with all these horrible people. I justified my anger by telling myself that if he had not died, none of these bad things would have happened to me. Of all the people he could have left me with, my abusive half sister, who took over my care, was the worst. That was a big source of my anger. I did not realize until I was much older how angry I was.

Now when I see how my anger has run my life, it is overwhelming. I can see the connection between my anger in response to small annoyances. I thought my anger was a volcano because its rage could burn and destroy anything in its path. At times I felt afraid to experience this rage, which is why I have never allowed myself to show my anger. Thus, I never got to process my anger properly and allow healing.

The Story of My Abuse

I want to share this part of my life story because of the many ramifications of my trauma on my life experience and my anger. I also want you to know that, regardless of what happens to you throughout life, you can still rise. You can shine when you have ways to release your trauma. This is possible for anyone who has lived through trauma as I have.

After my father's death, I was too busy simply trying to survive to grieve fully. Right away, my world turned upside-down. My status suddenly changed from a sister to a slave for my half sister and her husband.

Sopha told me that my job was to clean the house, cook, and fill up the water tanks every morning and every evening. I was not to talk or ask any questions, and I was not allowed to speak unless spoken to. I was criticized for the way I walked, sat, and talked, the way I chewed my food, and if I sat the wrong way, she would smack me. So, I felt that my entire existence annoyed her. If I did not get my chores done before she came home from work, I would be punished. This was true for my brother as well.

We had to wake up before the chickens, which meant around 4:00 or 5:00 a.m. I had to cook rice and clean the house. We did not have running water, so my brother and I hauled water from a well to fill the water tanks—it took about five trips back and forth. I was a skinny little girl, but I had to carry two water containers over my shoulders—a total weight of thirty to fifty pounds, each trip. My brother and I had to do this twice a day—once in the morning and then again right after school.

I was never to be late home from school. Not even one minute. When Sopha came home from the farm, I was supposed to have cleaned the house and made everything ready for her. If I was late from school, she would stand right in front of the house, waiting for me. Her hand would be hidden behind her back, where I knew she held a stick to beat me with. Just the sight of her standing there waiting for me would make my feet freeze in my tracks, my hands shake, my body tremble, and my heart pound fast. I'd be overwhelmed by fear of what was about to happen to me.

Then she would talk to me about why I was late. She would accuse me of all kinds of things—things I didn't even understand. One day I was late and there she was again, standing in front of our house with her hands behind her back.

"Did you spread your pussy on the side of the roads to get a fuck before you came home?" she asked.

I was ten years old! I didn't even know what that meant, but I felt so dirty and so worthless—unwanted. I felt disgusting, and I could not comprehend what had happened to me. My brother, Mhee, and I were both equally abused psychologically and emotionally, but he endured more physical abuse than I.

My sister was particularly nasty toward Mhee. She would yell anything she could think of. She threw objects at him daily—pots, pans, knives, anything within her reach. A bucket, a spatula, her bra. One time, she put her underwear over his head to humiliate him. I remember Sopha would regularly chase my brother with a knife down the street and around the village. The other siblings who lived nearby witnessed it, the neighbors witnessed it, but all they did was yell and tell my sister to stop.

However, no one physically stood up and intervened. All they said was: *Here we go again. Those two poor kids dealing with the crazy sister.*

Nobody tried to stop it. That was our abuse, every day. Those experiences taught me I was not good enough to be loved, I did not matter, my life was not important, and I didn't have a right to exist in this world.

I was just a child trying to survive the abuse. My childhood was stolen.

MY PERSPECTIVE OF MEN

While Mhee and I endured all the abuse physically, emotionally, verbally, and psychologically, my brother-in-law did nothing. He would listen and witness everything my half sister did to us, but he never once stood up or tried to stop his wife or defended us. He just sat there, silent. I realized then that I have no respect for men who show no strength or backbone. That experience shaped the way I look at men, especially men who resemble my brother-in-law. In my memory, he was the man with power, but he did nothing to help.

One time I was serving food to the grown-ups, which is expected of children in my family's culture. Children are supposed to do household chores and serve the adults food. The kids have their chance to eat only after the adults have finished eating. I was serving food to my brother-in-law and his friends. I stood around waiting to be told what to do.

Sometimes my brother-in-law would tell me "Go away," or, "Do not stand around." The first time he decided to speak up, he insulted me. "I can smell your pussy from here!"

Here we go again, I thought. I felt so dirty and so worthless!

Finally, he had decided to say something, but it was not helpful. Because of that experience, to this day I still have a reaction to men who show a lack of character or courage. My reaction is anger and disappointment. It does not apply to all men, but I have a hard time trusting men to be there for me or defend me. At times, this interferes with my relationships with men.

For many years of my adulthood, I would date men for only about six or eight months before I'd start to feel uncomfortable. I'd lose patience and be quick to leave the relationship if the man failed to meet my expectations. I'd sabotage the relationship, becoming withdrawn and distanced, which led to the end of most of my relationships with men. Of course, I did not do that intentionally. It was my subconscious fear of being let down or disappointed. I ran away from relationships before they turned into anything more.

From all the abusive incidents when adults watched yet did nothing, I formed resentment toward men, resentment toward people who abuse their children, and resentment toward men who show any sign of cowardice. I absolutely hate that.

Nobody Heard Me

During those times of abuse, I was surrounded by my other siblings. They were all grown-up people who had more power, more authority to change something. But all they did was casually *almost* suggest to my abusive sister not to hurt my brother and me. They watched and looked helpless when they could have helped. They could have helped a lot. I think they did not try hard enough. They would shout and yell at my sister to stop, but nobody intervened; no one took us to safety.

I felt so alone and abandoned by my own family who had more power and authority than they were willing to use. They let it all happen and were passive. It left me with a bad taste about a grown-up who has power and watches abuse but does nothing to stop it.

Yes, the feelings of abandonment, isolation, and loneliness cut deeply into my soul. I felt again as though I did not even matter. I did not exist. Even though I cried, yelled, or screamed, nobody helped me, so it seemed as though nobody heard it. I remember sometimes I would hear my sister's voice in my head telling me to jump off a cliff.

A scary thought is that I might have done so because I was so terrified of her. I was screaming inwardly because I felt like I could not speak or talk. I could not even ask for help. In my mind, I was yelling and screaming at the top of my lungs, but no one could hear it. It seemed like I was living in a glass container, and everyone saw me struggle, but nobody could hear my pain. I felt absolute loneliness and helplessness – more than anyone could imagine.

Because no one who witnessed the abuse I endured for years did anything to stop it, it taught me that I was worthless, I did not matter, and I might as well not exist. Those feelings alone caused a big hole in my heart and in my soul. They angered me. I felt absolute loneliness, pain, disappointment, and anger.

My Trauma From Abandonment

My experience of abandonment was not temporary. It formed the foundation of my life. It continues to be a shadow I cannot escape. Even though my life eventually turned out great, I still feel fundamentally alone sometimes.

When things have gone wrong, even little things, I've felt like no one would defend me; therefore, I would be triggered and put my guard up, ready to defend myself. The experience of abandonment has scarred me. I consciously and subconsciously feel abandoned and alone in this world.

The purpose of sharing my experience with you is to acknowledge that abandonment has long-lasting effects on a person's life. It is a traumatizing experience. I would say feeling abandoned is one of the biggest voids in my life. It continues to follow me, regardless of how many friends I make, regardless of how many people have come into my life. I still feel alone. I still feel abandoned in some ways. So it is a really scary thing.

When I had arguments with my current husband, for instance, and was met with the silent treatment or being ignored, my brain would automatically go to the feeling of being abandoned, which then triggered my trauma brain/survival brain to react. My trauma response is often anger, known as the *Fight Response*. Sometimes I withdraw or physically run away, known as the *Flight Response*.

Now, I am more knowledgeable. With more experience, I can recognize where my reaction came from; therefore, I know how to move past it. Abandonment causes trauma, and it is absolutely one of most helpless experiences in my life. As a mental health clinician, I know we can learn to cope with trauma-induced experiences (trauma response symptoms), but traumas change the landscape of a person's brain and their perception of the world.

Think of the brain as the surface of the Earth, which is beautiful and serene. Then a trauma occurs, like a volcano erupting, and it forever changes the landscape. We can never undo trauma, regardless of the number of treatments or the therapeutic method being applied. But treatment does help a person break out of being a victim of the trauma-induced responses.

We can become more informed, more aware, and more prepared to handle the symptoms of trauma. Trauma will not disappear entirely. Just as the volcano changed the landscape of the Earth, traumas change a person's blueprint in the brain.

ESCAPING THE ABUSE

At the time I graduated sixth grade—which is considered sufficient education in my village—my teachers and many people in the school community knew I needed to continue with higher education. I was one of the smartest kids in the school, as was my brother. I loved school. Even though I had to focus on surviving day to day in my abusive home, I excelled at school.

School was my happy place; however, I continued to feel small and not important compared to other kids. I felt so small as a human. I was the poor little girl who had no clean clothes to wear. I didn't want to be in front of the class because everyone would see me and laugh at me. So in classrooms, I would hide in the back, trying not to raise my hand or ask any questions—trying not to be noticed by classmates who would bully me.

There was one person who validated my existence, and she showed me kindness: my sixth-grade teacher, Manee Phasomthong. She was my first female hero. She would notice me, and she would make an effort to come and say hi to me and check in on me, making sure I knew that she saw me.

That meant a lot, and it felt so good to be noticed and validated. Teacher Manee would take the time after class or during lunch to provide support for me doing homework or asking me about my life.

Shortly after I graduated sixth grade, sure enough, my sister said I had had enough education and it was time to work for my food. News spread, and my teacher found out that I wasn't going to continue with school. She took initiative and convinced a majority of teachers—about fifteen, including the principal—to show up at my house asking my sister to let me attend high school.

Manee knew that something needed to be done, and she took action while other teachers tried their best to chime in. Of course, my sister denied their request. The teachers asked me what the reason was for my not attending further education. I was barely twelve years old, so I told the truth: "My sister won't allow me to go to school."

That was it. A group of teachers tried their best but left disappointed. As soon as they left, my sis was so angry at me for "embarrassing her in front of teachers," she grabbed a medium-sized stick of firewood and hit me repeatedly on my head while yelling, "This is what you get for humiliating me!"

I felt as though all the brains in my head crumbled and were destroyed, but somehow the most painful thing I experienced in that moment was her words. I was traumatized psychologically and emotionally, whereas my physical body went numb.

Some time passed after I graduated sixth grade. I was alone, and I didn't see any direction or future for myself. I thought that was how it would be for the rest of my life.

One fateful day, I was alone, cleaning the house and preparing food before my sister came home. I heard a motorcycle. Shortly after, I heard someone called my name. I heard, "Boonmee! Boonmee!"

I had to pause and think a little while because I did not recognize the voice at first. I remembered thinking to myself: *Who would be calling my name at this time?* I looked out the window and saw my teacher. She asked if my sister was home, and I said not yet.

"Go to your room and grab your clothes and come with me—hurry!"

I did not even give it a second thought. In that moment, I knew this was what I must do. It was a leap of faith I had to take. I went upstairs, got two T-shirts and one pair of shorts. Then I hopped on the back of her motorcycle. There I went! I took a leap of faith, and I left my abusive sister at the age of twelve.

CHAPTER THREE

The Branding of Poverty

Photo credit: Ryan Balow

I want to shed more light on the nature of poverty. It is not just a socioeconomic status; it is a personal status. Poverty has caused such deep scars and trauma in my life that persist beyond the abuse that I endured from my sister. Poverty is not just having no food, it is not just having no shelter, it is not just having no clean clothes to wear – poverty is branded into a person's soul.

"THE GIRL WHO EATS SHIT"

Growing up, I was bullied throughout school simply because I was poor. My clothes had holes and stains on them. My brother and I never had new clothes. We had to wait for donations from the government once a year to get a new school uniform. Sometimes we had to walk barefoot to school because we could not afford flip-flops, let alone bicycles. When I said *walk to school* I mean, like, five miles roundtrip every day.

We were some of the poorest people in my village. I had to share lunch with my brother, and our lunches were very small. Sometimes it was one egg to split; sometimes it was rice and a small fish. On a day of rice and fish, there was not enough fish, so we had to eat everything – including the fish gut, which still holds the waste matter the fish hasn't voided before dying. A group of students who witnessed my brother and I eating fish guts, started to laugh and yelled for the whole lunchroom to hear, "Hey, Boonmee! Boonmee the girl who eats shit."

This is when I got my new reputation at school. A group of students all began to chant and call me *Boonmee, the girl who eats shit*. Then, they turned it into a song they sang at the top of their voices through the hall. This was one more way I was branded with poverty. I find that life keeps finding a way to show you your place over and over.

After I left my hometown, I was with a friend at the convenience store, and I wanted to buy a can of Pepsi. At that time, I had finally earned my own money and could afford my very own can of Pepsi. I was short by less than two cents. I looked at my friend, and without any hesitation, she was taunting me, saying, "Wow, you are truly a poor person!" She then continued, "If I were to drop these two cents down the toilet, you would probably stick your hand down to get it."

In the same moment I was thinking: *Wow, finally I can buy my own can of pop!* my pride was taken away in front of everyone in the store. Worse yet, if she had dropped those two cents down the toilet, I probably *would* have put my hand in the toilet to get them out.

That incident still scars me today. Because of it, I developed a lot of anger around money, and I became very sensitive about money. I became cautious to make sure I would not be a burden to anybody in my life, to make sure that I would never allow myself to be made of fun like that, ever again. Once again, poverty was branded into my soul.

I have so many more stories about poverty and how I was branded as *a poor person* instead of *a person who lives in poverty*. I recall when I got my first job in Bangkok City, Thailand. I was a waitress in a small Chinese noodle shop. I served clients their noodle soup, making $150 a month. I barely made a living and paid my rent.

I remember I was so hungry, but I did not want to spend money to buy extra food beyond what the owner provided me. I secretly ate the leftovers from clients so I could have more money for something else. On one occasion, I got caught by the restaurant owner's son. I was so embarrassed and felt less than other people.

Poverty causes such a deep scar on a person's soul. It has caused so much turmoil in my life, in marriages, in my relationships, and has made me cautious and sensitive about money. Our society does not talk enough about the ripple effect of poverty on people's lives. Poverty causes trauma. The majority of my life journey has been trying to prove my worth, trying to make sure I am not a burden to other people.

My Love-Hate Relationship With Money

Money, and the lack of it, caused anger in my life. Money was the reason I ended up sleeping on the street in Bangkok, Thailand. I was about fifteen years old. I was visiting my brother for the weekend. I needed money for a bus ticket; it was roughly fifty cents to go back to my factory's dorm in which I resided. The dorm closed at a certain time. I did not have that fifty cents.

I asked my brother for the money, but he didn't have any money left until his next paycheck. I called people I knew to borrow money, but no one was able to help me, so I started to walk. From my brother's apartment to my factory was about fifteen miles. Of course, I did not make it back on time, so I ended up sleeping behind an ATM machine on the side of the road. As a young woman of fifteen, I was scared and terrified that I might get raped by a stranger, so I hid and disguised myself as best as possible. That was another moment in my life I told myself I never, ever wanted to be in again.

Presently, I am not only surviving but thriving. I make my own money. I am a successful person in all aspects of life. However, the effects of poverty still lurk, especially when I've gotten a job offer, and I know it's not a fair offer. Not only do I feel angry, but I feel underserving all over again. Poverty significantly impacts a person's perspective and sense of self-worth.

Money was one of the reasons I left my wonderful ex-husband. I was required to sign a prenuptial agreement before I married him. This was perhaps the most significant moment when money caused anger in in me. I was required to prove my intent so I could marry. I didn't realize how much it bothered me until some time after being married. After five years, I decided to leave my husband solely because of how people looked at me, or at least, I assumed they saw me as *the neighbor's Asian wife* or *that gold digger*. You know, I felt I was being criticized for how much money I had or where I came from.

To live believing everyone around me was judging me based on whether or not I had money was traumatizing. It tore at my self-confidence and self-worth. I had a hard time with that. I tried, to the best of my ability, to contribute to my marriage—being a good wife, cooking and cleaning, and being loyal to him while I was a full-time student with a side job here and there—but it was not enough to make me believe that I was an equal partner. I decided to leave the marriage and start all over on my own.

Since the divorce, my ex-husband and I have maintained a good relationship. I took him out for lunch to thank him for all the good times we shared, and at the end of the meal, we went up to the cashier to pay. I pulled out my credit card and the cashier looked at both of us and said, "Oh how nice—shiny credit cards. It must be nice to not have to lift a finger, just use your husband's credit card." A stranger made that comment to me! A Stranger! That comment made my blood boil.

Once again, I was reminded that who I am and where I've come from is nothing more than poverty. Poverty is not just my status; it has become my identity. Slowly and subconsciously, I transformed my identity from *a person who comes from a poor family* to being *a poor person*.

This statement cuts deep into my soul. Poverty stains my self-worth and self-confidence. Poverty also drives me to become somebody in the world. I do not want to be seen as only an Asian woman who married a white man. When I explained this to my ex-husband, he finally realized how much it had pained me, and he apologized. He told me he finally knew why I wanted to be on my own. I felt so relieved when I heard him apologize. Finally, he knew how important it was to me to be independent and stand my ground without a man.

SURVIVING SEXUAL ASSAULTS

As if poverty hadn't caused enough damage in my soul, I was constantly being preyed on by sexual predators. I never told anyone—not even my own family members—about the sexual assault I experienced. I don't know if it was because I was so traumatized or I was so busy simply trying to survive. I was terrified of being assaulted at the same time I was living the trauma of abuse and poverty. My first sexual assault was when I was about thirteen years old.

I was working for a time as a shampoo girl in a beauty salon, where I also stayed. My specialty was massaging clients' heads after their shampoo. I was good at my job. I got so many compliments from clients and sometimes made good tip money. In the salon, there were two ladies who were much older than I. They were incredibly beautiful, so they attracted a lot of customers—especially male customers.

One customer came from a big Bangkok city to work in the same town where the salon was. This client would come to get his hair shampooed a few times per week. He'd flirt with the two stylists, but I did not pay much attention. Some time passed. This client became acquainted with the other two women. One night, they told me to lock up the shop and said they were going to hang out with some guy friends. I did as they asked and then made my way to the residential part of the salon to turn in for the night.

Before I went to bed, I heard the sound of a truck pulling into the parking lot. I heard the doorbell and a familiar voice. I opened the door enough to see who was there. The client stood at the door and told me the ladies forgot something, and he had come to pick up the stuff for them. I was young and innocent, and I let him in.

He proceeded to look for something but seemed awkward in his manner. Eventually he told me to sit down on the couch. I didn't understand what was happening; I had been taught to do as adults told me to do. So I sat down. He sat close to me and started touching my body. He told me that he had been secretly admiring me, that he never liked the two ladies. He said I was the reason he came to the salon multiple times a week.

I froze, terrified; I could not scream or speak. He pushed me down on the floor and laid his body on top of mine. I started to scream, and that was when he took out a knife. He said I could trust him—he said he was *a good person*—and if I didn't believe what he said I could hurt him. He then put a knife in my hand while he grabbed my hands tightly.

Before he managed to undress me, I heard a motorcycle approaching like a miracle. It was the two ladies returning. The client quickly gathered himself and left. The next morning, I told the ladies what happened to me, and I said I was scared.

"How was it?" they asked. "Did you like it?"

I said he did not get inside of me. One of them said, "Are you sure? You look pale." Then they giggled about it.

A year later, I left the salon and moved to Bangkok city. I was walking down the street one evening, about to grab some food from street vendors. It was a holiday of some kind, because the street was empty and quiet. I noticed a man on a motorcycle, wearing a black helmet. He managed to show me that he had a weapon. Immediately I knew I was in danger.

I started to walk faster but, on a motorcycle, he was faster. He jumped his bike onto the sidewalk and followed me, hunting me down. I ran for my life for two miles before I saw a hotel and ran into the lobby. I sat there the whole night before I felt safe enough to walk back to my apartment. That experience was the first time I felt being a woman is not safe.

Sometime after that incident, I got a job at a tourist attraction district. I was a salesperson at a gift shop. My boss, an arrogant man, was rude and he disrespected women. He would try to get into any female staff member's pants, including mine, but I made it clear to him that I hated him. So his way to punish me was to set me up for his VIP client. At this point, I was about sixteen years old.

My boss told me the VIP client made a huge purchase, so we ought to provide the best service possible. He ordered me to deliver the product to the client's hotel. I did so because it was my job, but for some reason the client told the hotel staff to escort me to his room. I immediately felt uneasy and trapped. Once I was inside his room, the customer acted weird and blocked the door the entire time. He then cornered me in every way, shape, and form.

My gut told me I was in danger. So I decided to play along and told him that I would really appreciate it if he would bring me a glass of water. In the ten seconds it took him to get the water, I ran out of the hotel room.

When I worked at a factory, I lived at the factory's dormitory. The quality and the safety of staff was not regulated, to say the least. Lodging in the dorm was included with the job, but nothing separated the males' and females' dorms. Male residents stayed on the second floor, females on the third. Every night I would go to sleep in fear of getting raped because it happened frequently to others.

In the middle of the night, a group of men would come up and watch the women sleep. Sometimes, they'd target one woman. Sometimes, a man would fondle a woman from behind while she was sleeping. I never allowed myself to go into full, deep sleep. I spent most of my nights pretending to sleep or disguising myself in between two other females, so I'd be less likely to be targeted. There were no workers' rights; there was no HR protection. Many of us were underage and some were illegal immigrants. So we were told if we wanted a job, we needed to keep quiet.

I was living in fear, and I escaped as soon as I could. Somehow I managed to survive all of these experiences but not without trauma. Trauma from sexual assault happens way before intercourse. The process of being raped is the most terrifying and most traumatic experience for victims. I hope that the stigma around sexual assault and victim-blaming stops. Victims are accused of *asking for it* or blamed for causing rape and assault because of the way we dress or how we act. The truth is that the cause of sexual assault or rape is, 100 percent, caused by rapists, period.

LEARNING TO BELIEVE IN MYSELF

While I was surviving abuse, surviving poverty, surviving sexual assault, I somehow managed to pursue my education. Deep down, I had the sense of knowing there was something more to life than hardship. I knew I must survive. I knew there was a greater plan for me on this Earth; my intuition told me that I was meant to be more in this lifetime. I could feel there was a bigger purpose for me to be on this Earth than simply surviving.

I told myself: *If I have survived all these terrible things, I must be someone who will do great things in life*. This belief formed yet another identity and characteristic of mine: *Determination and Grit*. Because of that belief, I kept telling myself—especially when I faced difficulties or hardship – one day I would be someone of influence and bring positive change to the world we live in.

Throughout my journey, especially during those difficult moments of surviving painful experiences, I came up with a conclusion or diagnosis about myself in a particular way. This internal self-evaluation or self-diagnosis was that I formed specific characteristics needed to survive those painful moments.

The Journey Within

Over the span of our lives, we encounter many difficult events and try to make sense of events and circumstances around us. So we form our identity and personality traits. This process of surviving varies from person to person. In my coaching business, I coined the term *Identity-Stamps/Identity-Blueprint.* They can be defined as an individual's internal-dialogue or diagnosis to oneself. Identity stamps are created through the process of surviving, or efforts to survive, painful moments or hardships. We create an internal-belief/diagnosis about our own capability or the lack thereof. This identity-stamp is rehearsed over time and creates an internal blueprint in a person's subconsciousness.

In my life-coaching business, I use the Identities Mapping process to uncover clients' internal dialogue

(Identity Stamps) that they hold as their truths. These truths can, at the same time, cause blind spots that prevent you from becoming who you want to become. They can prevent you from achieving your goals.

Another important concept I want to recognize is the *power of will*. Regardless of how helpless I was, how alone I felt, and how scared I was, I never lost my will to survive.

The source of my will to survive is *Hope*. Hope gives me the willpower to keep moving forward. It comes from my *Belief in Myself* that I am meant to be someone in this life. Hope gives me the willpower to keep on fighting.

I formed a strong belief in myself to continue looking up and into the future. I somehow recognized that I had to keep hoping and believing I deserved better. I recognized that the only way out from the helplessness and hopelessness was indeed to keep hoping for a brighter future.

Why? What choice did I have from being on the bottom beside forward and upward?

If I focused my attention on my pain and my sorrow, all I could see and feel were the sorrow and the pain I tried to avoid. It was a vicious cycle. I honestly believe that we human beings are capable of cultivating this sense of knowing and belief in ourselves. We must learn to listen to that sense—to our intuition and gut feelings—that has kept us alive and safe so far.

Listen to that inner voice, the one who guides you, especially the voice who has kept you safe from dangerous situations. Some might wonder how to develop and believe in intuition. Well, look back to the darkest moments in your life. Reflect upon the very thoughts and decisions that helped you escape or survive that situation. We often seek answers from outer places instead of from within. If you slow down and listen to your intuition, you might find that the answers you need lie within you.

CHAPTER FOUR

A Light in the Cave

THE VICIOUS CYCLE

I am the youngest of twelve in my family. My brothers and sisters have all ended up in the same cycle that has persisted for ten generations. Most of them went to school only until fourth grade; a few gained sixth-grade diplomas. Most children in my hometown can expect no higher than a sixth-grade education because they are needed to work on the farms. Families cannot afford the cost of sending their children for more education; nor can they afford to lose the laborers on the farm because it means less rice or produce for the family to survive on. Education is not accessible for everyone because education is not a right; it is a privilege.

After the harvesting season, most of us in my village would migrate into the bigger city, Bangkok City, to earn our living and send home money to our parents and families. When we ran out of jobs, we'd go back home and do farming. We'd grow rice, tapioca plants, or sugarcane, or raise buffalo to support our livelihood. Generation after generation, nothing has changed. Observing this, I felt uninspired to follow that path. I did not want to continue that vicious cycle.

I didn't know how I would do it, but I knew I would not live that way. *Having a degree in higher education is the key to getting out of poverty,* I thought. However, as I watched all my siblings enter that cycle, stopping at fourth or sixth grade, I thought my future was predetermined. I felt helpless—the sort of helplessness in which you believe you cannot make decisions about your own future.

I believed if I had a college degree, it would allow me to access a different kind of job—better income and better opportunities. I needed to take a leap of faith and keep pursuing my education.

My Brother Saw My True Potential First

My biological brother, Mhee, and I have a special bond, especially through education. Without saying it, we both knew as children that school was our happy place. When we were back home, we were busy surviving the abuse, poverty, and all those responsibilities and chores. We did not really have many happy moments or happy memories together outside school. School was our happy place.

My brother graduated from sixth grade. Of course, we knew we could not afford for him to go to school. We needed a scholarship. So, he applied for a private scholarship, and he got it. The scholarship would allow him to pursue his education as far as he needed or wanted. It was a generous scholarship.

A year afterward, I graduated from sixth grade. I won a scholarship that would allow me to have higher education; however, the scholarship committee decided to give the scholarship to another deserving student. I was told there were so many poor and deserving students, they preferred to give only one scholarship per household. Since my brother had received his scholarship the year before, they said they would give the scholarship to other deserving kids.

That decision not only broke my heart, but my brother's heart as well. He knew I deserved to be in school. He wrote a beautiful, heartfelt letter to the scholarship donors asking them if they would please split the scholarship with me. He wrote about how deserving I was, how good a student I was.

I remember reading the letter from the scholarship donors stating how impressed they were with my brother and how inspired they were by a thirteen-year-old who knows the value of education. They were so impressed he was fighting not only for his education, but his sister's as well.

The donors granted the scholarship to both of us. They allowed us to split the money and said they would continue to support us as far as we wanted, even if it was in a program they hadn't heard of.

With joy and excitement, I told my sister.

"Nope," she said, "You are mine, and you belong in the kitchen."

That devastated my brother and me.

I believe my brother felt so deeply hurt that I could not have the same opportunity, he did not complete his education. Fast-forward, he ran away from high school because of it. But today, I am immensely proud of him. He is pursuing his own bachelor's degree while having three kids and a wife to care for. He struggles through life to make ends meet, but he is now the owner of his own printing company. He is still pursuing his bachelor's degree.

Education is our special place, our bond. I must admit, though, that academically he was the smarter student. School was a source of joy for us both. Not only did we get to escape from the abusive sister, but in school, we could express our interests and learn about life outside our village.

The First With a College Degree

When I was a girl and walked to school, just the sight of the school building made me feel immediately uplifted and inspired. I knew education was my calling. I knew that education was my *magic wand* to get out of poverty and create the life I wanted. I had a sense of knowing, a sense that I belonged in school, and a sense that I needed to keep pursuing education. Yes, I was daydreaming about having a college degree and becoming somebody in this world. I kept that excitement and joy quietly to myself.

I see education as a gift and a privilege. It is a key to many opportunities. Sometimes I find that young people do not have that sense of gratitude or recognition of their privilege for having access to education. I want to remind people that *education is a privilege.* We need to embrace and be grateful for the opportunity and access to equal education.

TRANSFORMATION AND TURNING POINTS

There are a few people I've met who helped me during major turning points in my life. The first are a couple I met through my GED school.

I was still pursuing my GED at nineteen years old. Getting my GED was a long journey, as I had to move around and work a variety of jobs. However, I continued to pursue my education. During that time, I was located in Bangkok, Thailand.

After working all week, I'd go to a community education center located in the basement of the police station. I'd learn about various subjects and meet the diverse people who taught. Two of the teachers were a couple from Thailand originally, but who grew up and lived in Australia. They returned to Thailand wanting to give back, wanting to make a difference in society. They chose to teach English to underserved students—you know, people like me who were pursuing their GED. That is how I met them.

With only that brief interaction, this couple somehow saw something in me, some potential that meant I could do more in life. That was the beginning of a turning point. They helped me believe I could make a difference in my life as well as in the lives of others. I think that was the first time I recognized my true potential. I knew then that I wanted to help people for the rest of my life.

I understood then my lasting desire was to bring people like you hope, to help you find your true purpose in life, your true happiness, in whatever way, shape, or form. And I have continued to do that in my own way, every day, since.

As I mentioned, I first met this husband and wife through the informal education program I attended to learn writing basic English. One day in class, they took me aside and talked to me, which surprised me. I didn't know what they were talking about, to be honest. They said a bunch of words I had never heard before, such as *transformational*. They told me I could do more in life, that I could become somebody and accomplish all I could dream of.

None of the words they used resonated with me at the time. But something about that couple made me believe in what they said. I could feel it in my gut and know it by my intuition. I told myself I needed to figure it out what it was they were talking about.

Even though I didn't understand what they were talking about when they referred to a *transformational seminar,* I took a leap of faith and followed them the following weekend to the transformational seminar called the *Landmark Forum*. I completed the transformational seminar and continued to a leadership program. I was promoted as the youngest seminar leader. My image of myself changed from being *the girl who has no sense of direction to the girl who can accomplish anything*.

Pay It Forward

I felt inspired at the end of that first transformational seminar. I had this urge to do something for myself, but I didn't know what it would be. I didn't know what I would get out of the seminar, but within me, I could hear a voice telling me it was something I needed to do. So I talked to the couple about having no money. I asked if I might borrow some from them and told them, "I would do anything to pay you back."

After conversations with seminar managers, program managers, and among themselves, they told me, "Go ahead! You can take this transformational life-coach program."

I believe the couple pitched in some. The program manager told me I could take that course for free. For the first time, I felt I had a say about my future. No matter who I was and where I came from—no matter how poor I was, how uneducated I was—I could still achieve whatever dream I had for myself. I was so excited and so moved by the possibility that I could become somebody in this world.

I felt such gratitude for the breakthrough and realizations I gained from that seminar, I told the manager, "I will work for my keep. I will do anything to pay you back."

I worked at my day job from 8:00 a.m. to 5:00 p.m. After work, I volunteered my time helping to set up the seminar room, to clean the bathrooms, to make phone calls, and to help promote this program in whatever way they needed. I did all that for free for two years.

From five o'clock until midnight, even on the weekends, I was making phone calls and traveling to talk to people about the benefits of the seminar, of this life-coaching program that I had completed. I wanted to share that possibility with everybody.

After I volunteered for two years, one day, the program manager called me into the office. I was so scared. I had no clue what was about to happen to me. He sat me down and said "Listen, you have been helping out for the past two years for free—what is it that you want?"

I said, "I am so grateful to be in this place—to know that my life matters, that I have a say about my future—so I do not ask for much."

And he put an application and placed that application package in front of me. He said, "I would like to offer you a full-time job."

At the time, for me to work in that worldwide company, leading seminars all over the world, I should have had a college degree. I did not even have my GED yet, but they offered me that opportunity. With tears on my face and my hand shaking, I signed the contract. That was my first job with a significant income.

It was also the first time someone asked me: *How much do you want for a salary?* I had no idea what to put down for a number; it was my first major job. It opened my eyes to whole new possibilities. It furthered my love for life coaching and transformational coaching.

I already touched base on this idea, but the theme that runs throughout my life is: *I am the one putting myself out there.*

Presented with so many good opportunities, had I not believed in myself or trusted myself, I would never have taken any of the chances given to me. I am grateful to myself that I continue to trust and believe in me. I want to highlight how important this piece is in healing and transforming the self. That is why I want to share this as part of my conversation with you, the reader.

Whether you believe in yourself and trust your judgment says a lot about how you relate to yourself. So many traumatic events happened at a young age and throughout my life. I survived the abuse of my sister, poverty, having to sleep outside hiding by an ATM, going without food, and attempted rapes through my early teens because I listened to my intuition.

When those events occurred, I never talked to anybody; I never once blamed myself. I never once internalized those bad things that happened to me as my own fault. I never once let those bad things that happened to me dictate what the future would hold for me. And that took a lot of courage, a lot of faith in myself and in life. My faith and belief in myself gives me strength, clarity, and inspiration to keep moving forward.

Regardless of what happens to you, regardless of how bad it is, how awful it is, as long as you *believe something greater awaits you,* you will be fine. You will keep moving forward. That is how I have lived my life so far. I just keep moving forward. I look to the future, not behind at where I've been.

This is my message to share with everybody.

Perseverance and Determination

I did volunteer for two years because I felt obligated. I did not do it because I felt like I owed somebody. I did it because I knew people would benefit from the program—they'd discover new possibilities once they found their true potential and their true purpose in life. I was so inspired by the possibility of making a difference in people's lives.

Sharing the life coaching program and the transformational seminar that I had gone through gave me such a great sense of empowerment. During those two years, I got so much. I was nineteen years old. I taught myself to speak English by reading five English sentences a day. I never went to school to learn to read or write English. I taught myself to simply recognize that I can be whoever I want to be.

A year after accepting my first position, I was promoted to interpret for a transformational life coach. I worked alongside an international seminar leader who would speak in English, and then I would translate what they said into Thai. I was able, without schooling, to speak a new language after the transformational seminar.

A year after that, I was promoted to seminar leader in the seminar leadership program. I was tasked with opening a new branch in a different part of the country. I started the branch from nothing. I opened the yellow pages and just closed my eyes and pointed to a name and dialed their number. I picked up the phone and started talking to people I had never met before. Two years later, I had increased the program from being completely unknown to enrolling two hundred people. And all this at the young age of twenty-three!

I became a registration manager in addition to being a seminar leader and was appointed to become the youngest worldwide international life coach and inspirational speaker. I was relocated to Singapore before I moved to United States. And that happened in a very short time. I was so young! And none of this would have been possible had I not gone to this transformational program.

My Ex-Husband

The next person to help me along my life journey was my husband for a time, Dave. I am forever grateful to him. He is one of the significant people who helped turn my life around.

Between 2006 and 2009, I was constantly training and practicing as a seminar leader, life transformational coach, and inspirational speaker. Every three months, I would travel to Japan. I have been to Japan over a dozen times to hone my skills in life coaching and seminar leadership training.

We met on one of those trips. I happened to sit next to Dave, and we started a conversation. He was on an educational trip to Thailand as well. He was a professor at a community college. He taught communication, and the purpose of his trip was to create an educational exchange program between the United States and Thailand.

Our sitting together was completely random, but I was so inspired by our conversation. I shared my life story with him, including how the seminar program had turned my life around. We exchanged phone numbers. From that point on, we started a long-distance relationship. We talked for two years, I believe, and then I relocated to Singapore.

Right about that time, my company was poised to send me to San Francisco, California, to be trained as a worldwide seminar leader and transformational speaker. I was twenty-seven years old. I decided to turn that down. Had I continued on that route, I can predict what my life would have been like. I would have been traveling around the world and doing what I enjoy. But at the same time, I wanted to continue exploring. I wondered: *What else is possible for me?*

Dave asked me to marry him and move to the States, which I did. I left Singapore and relocated to the United States in August 2009, and we were married for seven years altogether. Five years into that marriage, I left. Nonetheless, he was the first human being since my father who had loved me unconditionally. I could never do anything wrong in his eyes. He made me feel loved, respected, and like I was a perfect human.

I am forever grateful for that experience of sharing my life with him. Dave and I remain good friends to this day.

FROM ASIA TO AMERICA

Moving from Thailand to the United States was not in my life plan, for sure. To be honest, all I knew of the United States was from Hollywood movies that depicted New York City or Los Angles. But as we drove from the Minneapolis airport toward Rochester, my worry grew bigger and bigger while my excitement got smaller and smaller.

All I could see were cornfields and cows, which reminded me of the way I grew up. You could imagine my feelings and emotions. It seemed to me that no matter how far I had run from my hometown, it followed me. Seeing the rural landscape brought back my childhood and my hardships. When I arrived in Rochester, Minnesota, I experienced minor culture shock. I hoped and expected my life would be much better when I moved to the USA.

Nonetheless, it was a significant turning point in my life. This new chapter was not without challenge, of course. Compared to my earlier life, I was successful; had traveled and worked in many different countries, such as Bangkok, Japan, and Singapore; and had become an international life coach and inspirational speaker. But once I arrived in the United Sates, it was as if I was a nobody once again.

I did not feel I belonged or had a right to exist in this new country. I struggled to fit in and to be recognized as an equal. My experience and expertise were not recognized in the U.S. I was depressed for the first two years. I struggled to find my identity in this new country. Once again, it was as if I were starting my life all over. My first job was weeding gardens, helping farmers during the summer months.

Eventually I decided to attend a local college. I was scared because of my minimal ability to speak and write English. I had to lean in to my belief in myself and take a leap of faith. I turned hardship into an opportunity and continued my long-term dream of having a college degree.

This was when I developed another identity: *Conviction*. I shifted my mindset from *victim* to *victory* mindset. I sought and cultivated my strengths to navigate difficulties. Instead of counting my misfortunes, I counted my good fortunes.

I managed to graduate right on time with a high GPA—not without hard work, of course. I shed many tears, did lots of yelling and screaming, felt frustrated, and spent hours upon hours reading and translating words I had never encountered before. I found myself feeling most joyful and fulfilled when helping and empowering others.

I decided to pursue a career in psychology. After that, I moved on to a master's program in social work. I had attained the dream of helping people that would continue throughout my life. After graduating the master's program, I practiced as a mental health therapist and earned my certification as a Licensed Independent Clinical Social Worker (LICSW). My dream of education had finally been actualized.

I am now in the position where I can inspire others, especially young people, to pursue education, to embrace life's opportunities, and to be grateful for the privileges that we have. I am so grateful and happy to be where I am today. My belief in myself, my perseverance, and my faith give me the motivation to keep on moving forward.

CHAPTER FIVE

From Fear to Faith and Hope

FACING FEAR WITH TRUST AND FAITH

You have probably heard of having faith and trust in yourself before, from motivational speakers and on social media. I understood this concept at a young age. Although I did not have the proper term or way to describe it back then, I knew early on that I believed in myself. This belief in myself helped me learn to trust myself.

My successes so far are due to my belief in myself. Had I not trusted I could make good decisions for myself, I would still be stuck with my abusive sister. Had I not trusted or believed in myself, I would not have survived the abuse, sexual assaults, and poverty.

When my sister came after me, inflicting physical and mental abuse, the only way I made it through the insults and beatings was by turning to my source of inner strength.

That fateful day she beat me for being late was the worst day of my life, but it was also the day I found my bravery, the day I found my strength, and the day I formed belief in myself. I was tested many more times in my journey. I keep on moving forward regardless of what is coming my way.

Why? Because what choice do I have but to believe in myself?

What choice do I have besides moving forward?

What option do I have when I'm at the bottom but to move upward?

Not moving or not trying is not an option. This lesson translates into my life in a variety of ways. Having belief and faith in myself has helped me face my fears and learn to speak English. It helped me face my insecurity and write my first book. It gave me courage to share my most vulnerable moments for the entire world to know.

The moments I have felt the most successful are the moments I did not let fear stop me. Belief, trust, and faith in myself make up the compass I've used to navigate my life.

Start listening to your gut or intuition, believe in your judgment, and trust that you are stronger and braver than you think.

Putting Myself Out There With Faith and Hope

How do people develop faith and hope?

I can only answer for myself that I have strong faith and hope because I have gone through pains, disappointments, hardships, letdowns, hurts, and fears.

I observed my clients often struggle to have faith and hope in themselves or in their spirituality. This is because they look outward for answers and strength. They look for evidence outside themselves to have faith. What they do not realize is that faith comes from within.

Some of my clients focus on their past failures or past mistakes to justify their lack of trust in their judgment or faith in themselves.

I tell them, "You are looking at the wrong spot. Instead of looking at mistakes, you should look at moments of success and victories."

If this is the case for you, try to take note of who you were in a victorious moment.

What kind of mindset were you in?

What kind of a person did you have to be in those moments of success?

The moral of this story is this: You must learn to have faith, belief, and trust in yourself first; then you will learn to have faith in life and in those around you. Instead of looking at failures or weakness in yourself or others, practice seeing strengths and goodness in yourself and others. If you do that, you will find that life is wonderful and full of hope and promise.

I took a leap of faith when I ran away from my abusive sister with my sixth-grade teacher. I took a leap of faith and trusted my intuition when I enrolled in the transformational seminar. I took a leap of faith when I moved to United States. All these leaps helped me fulfill my dreams, become successful, help others, and influence them in positive ways.

Knowing My Purpose

Knowing your true purpose is the key to happiness. I focus on my true purpose often in my life and in my coaching business. I strongly believe that when we find our true purpose, we can move mountains. When you recognize your true purpose in life, then naturally you will be motivated and—better yet—be inspired to live life to its fullest. Everyday life becomes meaningful and purposeful.

As a mental health counselor at schools and universities, I have the privilege to work with young adults for whom life is still full of promises and wonders. However, I hear my students sounding confused and anxious about their future.

I ask many of these students, "Why did you choose to pursue education?" or "How did you arrive at your particular major?"

I hear answers, such as, "It's what we are supposed to do, go to college," or, "It's a way to make money." Very few answer, "It is my calling or my purpose."

Many people do not know their true purpose. I often observe students and clients are confused, lack motivation, and are not inspired by their future.

I remember the moment when I realized my true purpose is to help, to heal people, and to inspire people to live their life with purpose. This calling of mine has been the driving force to becoming somebody, to being successful, to having enough resources so I can help those in need. Knowing my purpose gives me a sense of passion for life. It gives me motivation and inspiration to make a difference in other people's lives.

Having a clear purpose and knowing my gift and what I am meant to do in this lifetime has taught me not to take life for granted – not to take my loved ones for granted. I celebrate small successes and moments. I count every small step of progress. I cherish every moment in life. I put effort into saying hi and smiling at strangers.

Sometimes small acts of kindness can go a long way. You might be the person who makes a difference to a stranger simply because you say hello or smile at them. Sometimes we think we need to wait until we have it all or until we become someone of importance before we help people. But what we don't realize is that small steps are part of the big success.

It takes one step at a time to climb a mountain. Do not underestimate the power of your kindness, your influence, and your contribution. If I had not taken those small steps, I would never have become the person I am today. Up until this point, I have been the only person in my entire family who left the country, who speaks in a different language, and who has a master's degree in a different culture, in a different language.

I am grateful for my loving, caring husband and my beautiful children. I have a beautiful home and I feel safe. I no longer settle for simply surviving; I want to thrive. I live life with happiness and joy while helping and healing people through my work. This results because I live life according to my purpose.

FORGIVENESS AND LETTING GO

Now we come to the most important journey of mine, which is the journey of forgiveness and leaving the past hurts and pains behind. I would never have been able to come this far in life had I not forgiven those who have hurt me, who have let me down, who have disappointed me in some ways.

Walking down memory lane and revisiting my past traumas, my painful memories, and my past hurts and fears, has not been smooth process, but it has been rewarding. I am now a new person, sharing my life journey through a new perspective. I am reflecting on what was the true magic wand that helped me move past my painful and traumatized experienced to become successful and thriving.

The answers are *forgiveness and letting things go.*

Forgiveness is a process and pathway to healing. Forgiveness begins from within. Forgiving is not forgetting. I cannot heal or transform if I continued to blame and resent those people who have done me wrong.

Why?

Because if I continued to direct blame and anger toward those people, I would have mentally and emotionally carried those people in my consciousness throughout my life journey.

How awful would that be?

So, forgiveness is a *must*. Many times, we struggle with forgiving those who hurt us because somehow, we believe that forgiveness equates to forgetting significant parts of our lives.

Sometimes we think that forgiving means that we let those people off the hook. But this is not the case. Forgiveness is about us.

Forgiveness sets us free from those jerks and assholes who hurt us. Believe me, I've been there. It took me a long time to finally forgive my abusive sister. It took me many years to forgive my cowardly brother-in-law for not protecting me. It took every scrap of courage and every bone in my body to forgive and have faith in men because I was sexually assaulted by men. It took me years before I could eat potatoes because they reminded me of poverty—in fact I still do not eat potatoes unless I am forced to eat them or if I have dinner at someone else's house.

Most importantly, I must forgive myself for holding on to anger and resentment for many years.

What does the forgiveness process look like?

How can one begin to practice the forgiving process for someone or something?

Forgiveness is hard work, and it is an ongoing process. Forgiving someone who has abused you, hurt you, and failed you is a spiritual journey. It is an uphill battle. It takes practice, patience, and a lot of compassion for yourself and those who wronged you.

Remember, forgiveness is a process, and we are never really done forgiving. We will have to continue to forgive those who hurt us every time we get triggered. It requires a lot of loving and kindness to forgive someone who has hurt you.

Forgiveness Activity

Take some time to ask yourself these questions:

How long have I held this anger, hurt, fear, and resentment?

Answer in detail: ______________________________

____.

What does it cost me to hold this anger, fear, and resentment?

Answer in detail: ______________________________

____.

What does it do to my happiness?

Answer in detail: ______________________________

____.

How does anguish and turmoil affect my physical health, my mental health, and my spirituality?

Answer in detail: ______________________________

____.

When you have written your replies, ask yourself more questions.

Has it cost me enough? If yes, how so?

Answer in detail: ______________________________

____.

Can I afford to lose more of my happiness?

Answer in detail: ______________________________

____.

How will I allow this turmoil to affect my mental and emotional health?

Answer in detail: ______________________________

____.

Perhaps, ask yourself these questions too:

Who else is affected by my resentment, anger, and hurt resulting from my past?

Answer in detail: ______________________________

____.

How does my past experience and trauma affect my loved ones?

Answer in detail: ______________________________

____.

How does my resentment affect relationships with my spouse and my children?

Answer in detail: ______________________________

____.

Letting Things Go

As I mentioned before, forgiveness is a process. It is hard work, but it isnecessary if you want to move on with your life. I learned that I could not thoroughly move on and start over until I fully forgave.

What happens after we forgive someone?

In my journey of healing and forgiving my abusers, I thought I was *cured* and free of traumas and hurts. But forgiveness is only part of the healing process. The other half is *letting it go*.

I sincerely believed I was done with my traumas and with my anger and resentment toward my abusive sister and brother in-law. But as time went by, I found myself being triggered by little things that I reacted to as though I was in a war zone.

This is another shade of trauma: it never disappears entirely, much like a volcano that permanently changes the terrain of the Earth's surface.

What do I mean by that?

I overreact to mundane scenarios. For example, when my husband and I first lived together in the house we bought, I expected he would magically know how I felt and know what I needed at any given time. When he didn't validate my experience, I'd tell him I felt sad or lonely, and I would feel so let down.

When he did not recognize changes in my mood or my needs, it triggered my old trauma of *I am not enough to be noticed* or *I do not exist in his eyes*. Of course, when that happened, my feelings were deeply hurt, and I felt so small, like I did not exist. In that moment, I went right back to being my ten-year-old self who felt abandoned.

Another example is that I am an external processor, whereas my husband is an internal processor, so our communication styles are opposite. I want to solve any problem head-on, right then and there, because I believe that life is too short to go to bed angry with unresolved feelings. My husband, on the other hand, likes to process his thoughts and feelings in his own private time and quietly in his mind.

So, you can imagine what our communication looks like. I ask him to solve the issue right at that very moment, and he goes silent, thinking about what to say and how to say it correctly. You can guess the rest of the story—once again, I feel like, *He doesn't care about our relationship as much as I do,* or he becomes silent. He doesn't tell me what he is thinking, so I feel *neglected and abandoned.* I react emotionally and dramatically. These are examples of when I reacted to mundane scenarios as though I was again in the exact moment when I first felt abandoned or let down. It is an inappropriate reaction to the present moment.

The point is this: Forgiveness is just one side of the coin. In order to profoundly move beyond past hurts and pains and move on with my life, I must learn to *let it go.*

What does it mean to truly let things go?

It means I must recognize when I react to current circumstances led by my previous experiences. I learned that a lot of my reactions and defensiveness comes from my past.

Why does letting things go matter?

Holding on jeopardizes my current life situation. It sabotages my relationship with my husband and with those I love and care about the most. Again, letting things go is also difficult. It takes practice, compassion, and patience for yourself. If you want harmony and peace in your life and in your relationships, you need to let things go. Here is how I practiced letting go.

Practice Letting Things Go

Observe yourself when you are being triggered or reacting to a new situation similarly to how you reacted in the past. Then, when you feel calm and ready to let things go, find a quiet place where you can feel safe and calm.

Start by closing your eyes, if you feel safe to do so, or imagine that you are sitting and relaxing while watching a calm and smooth-running river.

Then, reflect upon those moments when you overreacted and your past hurts and trauma were triggered. Start by acknowledging those feelings, whether they are anger, sadness, or resentment. I want you to take a deep breath in, breathe out, and imagine that you are breathing those feelings into a balloon.

If you were triggered by someone who reminded you of a past abuser, take a deep breath in, and then breathe out, imagining that you send that abuser or your pain into that balloon.

Then, once you have captured all the feelings, the hurt, the pain, the abandonment, the resentment, or the person who hurt you, imagine that you knot that balloon permanently. Imagine saying goodbye to those feelings and those people while releasing that balloon into the sky and watching it disappear into thin air.

Or:

Imagine you are watching a leaf floating along the smooth-running river. Close your eyes or imagine that you have placed those people and feelings on that leaf, and now you are watching it float by and disappear into the foreverland, never to return.

Use either of these letting go techniques whenever you need. Remember, it is an ongoing process, and you might have to practice letting it go many times before you are truly free from those feelings.

MY PURPOSEFUL LIFE

Clearly, I am still in the process of forgiving and letting go. As long as I am alive, I will be reminded of the past. It may be while crossing paths with someone who sounds like my sister, or men who act or sound like my brother-in-law, or when I am triggered and feeling rejected by my loved one.

The point is that none of these situations or people will have the same effect on me while I practice forgiving and letting it go. I am now a new person, I lead a new kind of life, and I am happy. My life journey leaves me with scars and blueprints in my soul, but it also teaches me to be the person I am today: a strong, compassionate, and kind woman who perseveres, understands, and is full of determination, conviction, and grit.

I love and embrace who I am. I am now able to accept and love myself fully and wholeheartedly. I am ready and equipped to help and heal people from trauma and to empower people to find their true happiness. Life is beautiful and it is still worthwhile. This journey of mine has made me the best clinician and life coach because I lived through those difficulties. I was able to bring myself out of poverty and transform my mindset from victimized to victorious.

I know what it was like to be in the darkness. Now I am in the light; I can see things clearer, and I see opportunities and solutions much quicker than I have in the past. I hope that my life story inspires you to have hope, encourages you to start believing and trusting in yourself, and teaches you to life live with purpose.

Life is precious, and we only have one chance to live, so make the most out of it. Expect more from life. Keep moving toward your dreams. Start to own your life and find your true compass. When you know your true potential, you may be amazed by how much you can accomplish and conquer and overcome.

I believe that this book sheds some light on the issues of poverty, abuse, domestic violence, and sexual assault. My hope is that it not only impacts us as individuals, but also impacts us as a society. When people are happy, healthy, cared for, and protected, we will have a successful and productive society ɜive person at home will bring their abusive .ty to work. As well, a hungry individual will productive at work and in society. Thus, know this: Domestic problems are societal problems. An individual's problem is a collective problem. This is because our society is a collective of individuals.

What Is In My Future?

I started my coaching business, called Above & Beyond Coaching, LLC, in Minnesota. I hope to continue to fulfill my life purpose, which is to inspire people to find their true happiness by finding their true purpose in life. I believe that a successful life is a life with purpose. I also do inspirational speaking, sharing my personal experience of how small acts of kindness can make a huge difference in people's lives, much like it has in mine. I am also passionate about helping people discover their blockages and blind spots that prevent them from achieving their true potential.

Regardless of what my future holds for me, I am certain I will continue to make a difference and instill hope, faith, and empowerment in people with whom I cross paths. My ultimate goals are that I want to be a part of solutions to end homelessness and hunger. I want to continue to contribute and help better our society in any way that I can.

I encourage you to live life with purpose. Start counting victories and blessings in your life because that is where the happiness comes from. Focus on your blessings, not your misfortunes.

If you are up for the challenge, I would encourage you to start making a difference in your own circle or community, such as volunteering your time to cook for a homeless shelter, donating supplies to a women's shelter, or buying a meal for someone or groceries for those in need. Extend helping hands and show kindness to people around you.

Conclusion

My intention for sharing my personal journey with you is so that you will walk away with a profound appreciation for life. Regardless of what happened to you, regardless of how many traumas or hardships you may have endured, I hope you still believe that life is beautiful and full of wonders and promises.

I know what it feels like to be helpless and hopeless at times, but we truly have a say about our own life outcomes. You have the power of choosing what kind of legacy you want to leave behind. I recognize that bad things do happen, and unfortunately bad things have happened so many times to good people. It happens every day, but I hope you do not lose hope and do not lose faith in yourself or life in general.

Keep on believing in yourself.

Keep on believing there is more to life.

Keep on moving forward. Do not stop.

Small progress counts. Just keep on moving.

I tell myself every day to have faith. That is one of the most important messages. There were times when I felt my efforts would not pay off, that my good deeds were not rewarded, and I felt defeated at times.

Most importantly, know that even in those moments of defeat, you are still making a difference by not giving up. The act of continuing on your path, on your journey, gets you over the hurdles and obstacles. You set an example for people who are watching you. Even if there's just one person, just one who looks up to you and admires you, you make a difference in that person's life. People who witness your journey will be inspired by you.

Practice believing in yourself and strengthening your faith—your faith in yourself, your faith in life, and your faith in religious belief. Find your true purpose. Strengthen your beliefs, develop your faith, and pursue your dreams. It is never too late, and it's never a right—or wrong—time to make a difference in your own life or the life of others.

Ask yourself these questions:

- *What am I here to do?*
- *What is my purpose in life?*
- *How do I know what my purpose is?*

I suggest you look back in your journey, on your past experiences—especially those moments when you found yourself feeling empowered, joyful, happy, feeling like you have accomplished great things, and so on. In those moments, you will discover your purpose.

What do I mean by that?

When I do something that is in line with my purpose, I feel so empowered, happy, energetic, and full of creativity and joy. Once you know your purpose, then act accordingly and fulfill that purpose. Once you find your life purpose, your life will be much simpler, easier, and rewarding.

Your purpose will serve as your compass in life. Do not get me wrong; having a purpose does not mean that you are not going to endure any more hardship or difficult times. You will, but it will not drag you off your path for too long. Your purpose will be the compass that corrects your course and keeps you on track. You may get distracted and fall off the path, but you'll always know where to return.

If I had not found my purpose in life—helping people by spreading faith, love, and hope—I would probably still be at a loss, without a sense of direction. So find your purpose. Start practicing believing in yourself, strengthening your faith, and speaking and acting according to your purpose. You will be successful and your life will be much more joyful, happy, and full.

Remember, small acts of kindness matter. A little act of kindness can profoundly change one person's life, much like my sixth-grade-teacher changed mine.

Do not wait until you *have it all* before helping someone, before making a positive change in your life and in the life of people around you. You have what it takes. Everybody is capable of kindness. Everybody has a power of influence to make a difference in this world. It does not have to be a big thing. Smile at the person walking down the street or sitting across from you on the bus. Or just ask some stranger how they're doing today, or donate money, time, or expertise to a worthy cause. Provide a meal for homeless people. Once a year, volunteer your time. Just continue to be kind.

Be kind as well to yourself. We are most happy and successful when we can contribute, when we can make a difference in other people's lives. That is my advice. Remind yourself of how wonderful your life is. Count the little blessings as well as the big blessings. Enjoy life. Do not take life for granted. Do not take things for granted. Just enjoy it.

Next Steps

To interact directly with Boonmee Pakviset McElroy, to schedule speaking events, or to set up personal Life Coaching sessions please visit:

www.aboveandbeyondcoachingllc.com

emails: boonmee18@yahoo.com, aboveandbeyondcoachingllc@gmail.com

Phone number: 507-202-7411

I dedicate space on my business website for you to share your personal experience and insight from reading this book.

art of my dedication to end hunger and ness, portions of the proceeds from this book will be donated to various organizations around the United States that help homeless people and people who are in great need.

Call to Action

Reach out to your local homeless shelters—women's or family shelters—and volunteer your time to cook, donate necessity items, or make financial donations, at least once per year.

Search for organizations of your interest that are in line with your personal values and passions. Please help support organizations that work toward ending the issues of homelessness, such as:

Walking With A Purpose MN

Walking With A Purpose MN is an outreach for the unsheltered community since 2014. Its mission is to help with the daily necessities of the unsheltered and to promote tiny home villages, based on community first, as a solution to chronic homelessness. The organization donates supplies and visits homeless camps around Minnesota multiple times per week. It is the outreach for *Settled*. (walkingwithapurpose.org, founder and president, Todd Feske)

Settled

Settled is part of the University of Minne Center for Design's tiny home project. *Walking With A Purpose* establishes tiny home villages, called *sacred settlements,* on church property. Sacred settlements are an innovative, research-based way to address long-term homelessness by developing holistic tiny home communities in cooperation with a faith community. Currently, they are looking for churches to host sacred settlements and others to sponsor the building of the homes to the homeless. Walking With A Purpose MN is always in need of donations such as camping gear, clothing, shoes, socks, canned food, and financial support. Please visit settled.org/sacred_settlement/what-are-they.

MICAH: Metropolitan Interfaith Council on Affordable Housing

MICAH lives out the prophetic vision "to do justice, to love mercy, and to walk humbly with God." (Micah 6:8). MICAH envisions a metropolitan area where everyone, without exception, has a safe, decent, accessible, and affordable home. Visit: https://www.micah.org/donate.

I know what it is like to experience and survive poverty; homelessness; emotional, physical, and sexual abuse. I understand how important it is for others to know that our past does not define us but can guide us to help others. I strongly encourage you to help others and practice your kindness when you can.

Please consider reaching out to women's shelters or family shelters in your area, and volunteer your time, donate money to the shelter, or donate necessary items for survivors of domestic violence and abuse at your local women's shelters, such as:

CADA

Providing safety and support to victims of domestic and sexual violence through education, advocacy, and shelter. CADA is always in need of donations, such as toiletries, clothing, shoes, socks, women's personal hygiene items, and financial support. Please visit www.cadaMN.org. Office (507) 625-8688 Ext.111. 24-hr Crisis Line: 1-800-477-0466.

About the Author

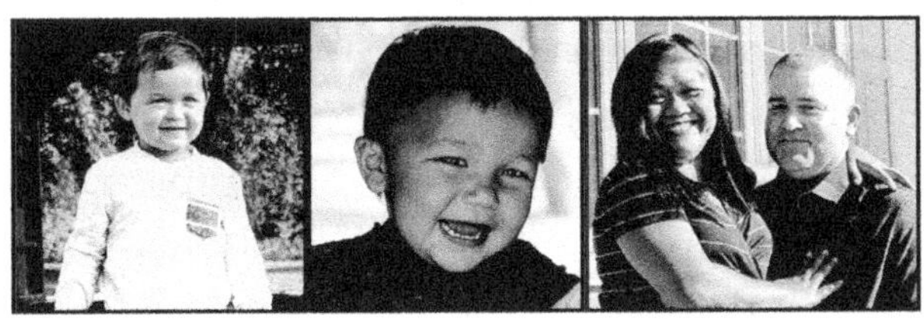

Boonmee Pakviset McElroy grew up in Thailand, where she lived and traveled between Thailand, Singapore, and Japan as an International Life Coach and Inspirational Speaker prior to moving to the United States in 2009.

Boonmee is a Licensed Independent Clinical Social Worker, Certified Trauma Focused Therapist, International Life Coach and Inspirational Speaker, Author, Minority Business Owner, and Mental Health

Counselor at a prestigious university in the state of Minnesota. Most importantly, she is a survivor of severe poverty; mental, physical, and emotional abuse; inhumane bullying; multiple sexual assaults; and being orphaned at a young age. Through all odds, Boonmee has persevered and become successful. She founded her own Life Coaching business: Above & Beyond Coaching, LLC, in Minnesota.

Boonmee is passionate about public speaking. Her main goal is to inspire people to believe in themselves and to have faith to keep moving forward with their goals. Her primary interest in Public Speaking is in schools and universities to speak about life and the consequences and rewards of our choices and to show others how to move toward happiness, healing, and self-acceptance.

Boonmee likes to empower her audiences by activating their pathways toward kindness, compassion, gratitude, and hope. It is her hope that her audiences will learn to trust their intuition, have faith, and practice self-belief and find their true purpose, which will bring them their true joy and happiness.

Boonmee is happily married with her handsome and most loving and caring husband, Mike McElroy. She is the proud mother of two beautiful and charming sons, Micah and Marcus McElroy. She is also a daughter, sister, and proud auntie. She enjoys her beautiful life and is blessed with many wonderful family members, friends, and neighbors. She enjoys working as mental health counselor as well as a Life Coach, helping clients and students find their true happiness.

She enjoys fishing, traveling, and spending as much time with her adorable children as possible. She also maintains a close and supportive relationship with her brother, and they continue to be each other's cheerleader.

Made in the USA
Las Vegas, NV
03 February 2022

42942678R00069